HOW TO WRITE A SCREENPLAY

STEP-BY-STEP

Essential Screenplay Format, Scriptwriter and Modern Screenplay Writing Tricks Any Writer Can Learn

Sandy Marsh

© **Copyright 2018 by Sandy Marsh. All rights reserved.**

This document is geared towards providing exact and reliable information in regards to the topic and issue covered. The publication is sold on the idea that the publisher is not required to render an accounting, officially permitted, or otherwise, qualified services. If advice is necessary, legal or professional, a practiced individual in the profession should be ordered.

From a Declaration of Principles which was accepted and approved equally by a Committee of the American Bar Association and a Committee of Publishers and Associations.

In no way is it legal to reproduce, duplicate, or transmit any part of this document by either electronic means or in printed format. Recording of this publication is strictly prohibited, and any storage of this document is not allowed unless with written permission from the publisher. All rights reserved.

The information provided herein is stated to be truthful and consistent, in that any liability, in terms of inattention or otherwise, by any usage or abuse of any policies, processes, or directions contained within is the solitary and utter responsibility of the recipient reader. Under no circumstances will any legal responsibility or blame be held against the publisher for any reparation, damages, or monetary loss due to the information herein, either directly or indirectly.

Respective authors own all copyrights not held by the publisher.

The information herein is offered for informational purposes solely and is universal as so. The presentation of the information is without a contract or any type of guarantee assurance.

The trademarks that are used are without any consent, and the publication of the trademark is without permission or backing by the trademark owner. All trademarks and brands within this book are for clarifying purposes only and are the owned by the owners themselves, not affiliated with this document.

Table of Contents

Introduction 6

Chapter 1: What is a Screenplay? 7

    Physical format 8

    Screenplay formats 9

    Feature film 10

Chapter 2: Television Screenwriting Considerations 19

    Drama 20

    Sitcoms 25

    Additional Tips to Keep In Mind 29

Chapter 3: How to Create Characters 31

    #5 – Think like an actor 43

    What else can we do? 45

Chapter 4: Creating a Rough Draft 46

    Develop the story idea: 47

    Create the pitch: 47

    Give it structure: 48

    Build a full story: 48

    Create a beat sheet: 49

    Write the script (finally): 49

    NEXT STEPS: 50

Chapter 5: Editing a Screenplay 51

Chapter 6: Tips for Success 57

Conclusion 64

Introduction

I want to thank you and congratulate you for purchasing the book "*How to Write a Screenplay: Step-by-Step | Essential Screenplay Format, Scriptwriter and Modern Screenplay Writing Tricks Any Writer Can Learn*".

In this book, you will find all of the information you need to begin writing a screenplay, the details on the specifics of the most common types of screenplays, tips on creating believable characters in your screenplays, how to create a first draft and get to work on editing and tips that have worked for the experts.

You will need the information in this book if you want to create a successful script that will catch the eye of producers to get it to the big screen.

To not develop your ability to write a properly formatted screenplay would be Hollywood murder to your career. Style is everything, and this book covers that.

It's time for you to create an amazing screenplay.

Chapter 1: What is a Screenplay?

A screenplay (also known as a script) is a written output made for a television show, a movie, a video, or a game. When it is written for television, it is also called as teleplay.

Screenplay consists of action and dialogue. Action is where a character is noted to do an action, and a dialogue is where the character is speaking. These two components make up around ninety percent of a screenplay.

What sets a screenplay apart from a stageplay are the use of sluglines. This designates where the scene takes place, and what time of day it is, along with the weather that is occurring at the time. These descriptions are important so that the director can make sure that the scenes are set up properly.

Physical format

Screenplays are printed very specifically. They are also all put together specifically as well. This makes it easier for a producer to get through a bunch at one time. They are generally bound with a cardboard cover and a back page to protect the script when it is handled. Oftentimes, the first copy of the script is the only copy. While it is backed up, it takes a lot of paper to print a script most times, so it is important to save where you can.

In America, the script is usually printed single-spaced on letter size paper. It is printed using 12 point courier font. When it is bound, it is bound using a three-hole punch and held together with two brads. One at the top and one at the bottom. This makes it easier to flip through the script quickly.

Reading copies, those which are distributed, are often printed double-sided to reduce paper waste. This is because there are often more copies that will need to be printed later on, and scripts already take so much paper to print anyway, that finding ways to cut down is a must.

Scripts can often be delivered electronically, but many companies require that a certain amount of copies be handed to the company, or at least mailed if travel is not possible.

Screenplay formats

Screenplays come with a certain set of standards that must be met. These standards are ones that help keep everything uniform and allow for easy reading. They form a sort of blueprint for movies and other screenplays. This also allows a company to distinguish those who take things seriously, from those who have a more laissez-faire attitude. There are software packages out there that can help assist with the formatting of screenplays. This makes it easier to ensure that you will have a professional looking piece to show prospective producers. SmartKey, the first screenwriting software, sent codes to existing word processors. However, the ones today have their own macro entities.

Feature film

If you intend to get a motion picture on the big screen, there are a lot of stipulations for how you have to write your screenplay. The headings, formatting, and spacing all have to meet a specific set of guidelines. While the guidelines may vary from country to country, they are all pretty similar in the fact that they have to be uniform. This is because the rate of transfer from page to screen remains around one minute. This gives a rough estimate of how long the piece will run when taken to the big screen. However, some things often get cut, so it is a very rough estimate.

Nevertheless, if you ever want anybody to not only read what you have written, but to truly take it seriously, you will need to stick to the rules in order to ensure that they have as few obstacles between them and getting to the heart of your story. In general, you can think of the concept of screenplay formatting as mainly an aesthetic choice to ensure that every page of your screenplay is as clear and legible as possible. Each script you turn in should always be written in 12-point, Courier font. This goes for movies or television.

The Slug: Luckily, the Hollywood script format is simple once you learn the basics. Every screenplay is divided into different scenes, each of which represents a different location that the story is viewed from. When a new location is introduced in a screenplay, it needs to be described in a specific way so that the person reading it can automatically picture three key pieces of information. They will need to know whether the scene is taking place inside or outside, the time of day it is and the actual location. Together, these three things form what is known as the slug.

Each scene introduction is going to be written so that it appears on a single line, which will include the location details as well as relevant information about the time of day. The majority of slugs will start with either EXT. or INT., meaning exterior or interior respectively. In general, a slug with start with EXT. or INT. and end with either NIGHT OR DAY unless the specific time of day is crucial to the scene. The only time this will not be the case is during parts of the script where the action is repeatedly cutting between two places or is moving through a number of locations, following a character who starts out from a location that has already been defined. For example: EXT. CAVE – DAY

If you have already introduced the cave in the previous example, then you could simplify by writing BACK TO CAVE.

If a character is moving throughout multiple locations inside a predefined location, such as a house, you can write the intervening slugs as KITCHEN or BEDROOM to maintain the flow of the story while still providing the reader with the details they need.

While not required, the slug often also includes the indicator SUPER which is followed by identifying information and indicates what would be superimposed on the screen for example SUPER: 10 years earlier.

If you are writing a conversation between two individuals who are not speaking to one another directly, you can use the indicator INTERCUT BETWEEN after both of the settings have been determined with a standard slug.

The shot: While the shot will also appear in capital letters with a similar type of formatting, it serves a different function when compared to a slug and shot not be confused with it.

As an example: ANGLE ON JACK, C.U. ON GUN. When writing your screenplay, you will use this technique to draw specific attention to an element of the action. It is typically followed by its own description, almost written as an aside, that is always ended with the indicator BACK TO SCENE before the action from the main scene resumes.

Action elements: An action element is going to come directly after the slug and is preceded by a blank line that runs the length of the page. The action element is responsible for setting the scene, literally, as it describes the setting. In it you will introduce what your characters are doing in the scene that will ideally naturally set the scene for what is going to come next. Any action written in this section should be written in real time, which means you are going to want to write as crisply and cleanly as possible in an effort to convey exactly what the audience will see on screen.

When you write your action elements, it is important to leave out as many extraneous details as possible as this makes the script easier to shoot as fewer unique props will be required. The only time you are going to want to go over the top with atmospheric descriptions is when the atmosphere is crucial to what is taking place on screen. For example, if you picture your favorite horror movie, you can bet that the scene that introduced the main location contain an action element with descriptive text.

However, if you are writing scenes that include lots of tense, back and forth dialogue, or action, then you are going to want to do your best to ensure descriptions are kept to an overall minimum. This will help to create an overall feeling of watching the scene play out in real time which naturally makes your script feel as though it could easily be adapted to the big screen.

In order to write action that plays on the page, the easiest thing to do is picture yourself having coffee with a friend and discussing something interesting you saw on your way to the café. This way you will be sure that you cut out all the filler and only focus on the parts that really matter. During these scenes, you are going to want to keep your paragraphs short, no more than five lines in a paragraph, no matter what. Be sure to capitalize any sound effects that are used. Between each paragraph you are going to want to leave two blank lines. By splitting up your descriptions and your action, you are adding an overall visual emphasis to your story, making it feel more like a movie throughout.

When introducing characters, capitalize the entire name, you are also going to want to include a specific gender as well as age. This information is not only going to be crucial when it comes to understanding what is going on in the story, but when it comes to things like budgeting and casting as well. Make sure you don't go so far as to describe specific hairstyles and clothing, except in situations where it is crucial to the plot. You are also going to want to avoid using parenthesis to indicate action when introducing a character. This means no: BOB (cracks a beer).

When describing movement, you are going to never want to use the word camera. Instead, replace it with the word we. This means no: the camera follows, instead it would be: we follow...

Setting up dialogue: The name of the character who is speaking is going to appear in all caps, tabbed in to almost the center of the page and then directly followed by relevant dialogue. The name of the person speaking can either be the name of the character (BOB) or a description if the person isn't known (MAN IN BLACK). Occupations are also acceptable if they are easily identifiable by the average person. If a character is going to play more than an incidental role in the story they should have a name. Be consistent when you refer to a named character, this means no calling BOB by his name in once scene and then by his last name in the next.

Writing Dialogue: The dialogue itself is going to appear located between the left margin, which is where the slug and the action are written and the margin where the character name is written. Writing good dialogue is certainly an art form all to itself, and most new screenwriters make the mistake of over-writing their dialogue.

The end result of this, in most cases is going to be dialogue that comes off more like a play than a movie, which tends to make scenes seem slower than they might otherwise be. It is important to try and keep your dialogue informal, while at the same time not stuffing it full of as much slang as you can manage. If it is important to the story that you character have a regional dialect, you can mention it when you describe them initially, but do not write out their lines in a regional dialect, unless it is a single line written in such a way to indicate emphasis.

When writing dialogue, it is important to make an effort to reflect the personality of each character in the things that they say, while also walking a fine line of not overdoing it. This will make it easier for the reader to picture the conversation as if it were actually happening, as opposed to two characters in a book, spouting soliloquies at one another. This also relates to the way in which key information is relied by the characters in the scenes. You should aim to express inner feelings in a subtle manner, without resorting to on the nose writing where each character simply says what they are thinking or feeling. Your overall goal should be to make the reader, and thus ultimately the audience, feel as though they are a fly on the wall for a real conversation.

Keep in mind that during almost all conversations, the primary players are rarely going to come right out and say whatever it is they mean. Instead, the conversation is going to have subtext. This means you are going to want to leave out bits and pieces of what exactly is going on and allow the audience the opportunity to figure it out on their own. Not only will this make the scene feel more natural, it will be more interesting to watch (or read) as well. For example, in the movie Jerry Maguire, the character of Jerry Maguire uses the phrase "You complete me" to indicate that he is finally ready to express his feelings for the romantic lead. In this instance, the audience knows he means he loves her because earlier in the movie there was a scene of a deaf couple using sign language and a discussion of the sign for love.

While this example is just a little thing, it still makes the audience think, which is a key to keeping them interested in what is taking place in front of them. As such, you are going to want to consider every line of dialogue that you write and the other possible ways that the same intent could be expressed without directly coming right out and saying it.

Parenthetical information: Any parenthetical information that you need to include in your script is going to appear left indented within brackets, underneath the character name. They are used only to express the emotion the character is currently feeling in the moment. For example, (laughing), (angry), or (upset). Any parenthetical information you provide should always be short, descriptive and to the point. As with any ancillary information, they should only be used when they are crucial to the plot.

Transition elements: Certain transitions are going to be optional, these include things like DISSOLVE TO: or CUT TO:. When you use them, they are going to need to be right indented, not flush right, and should only come after a blank line on the page and should always be followed by two blank lines as well. When you come to the end of page without completing a scene, the scene transition should always stay with the shot that was just completed which means you will never start a new page with either DISSOLVE TO: or CUT TO:, those would remain at the bottom of the previous page.

Transitions are primarily used to denote a major shift in time or location, and sometimes, like using MATCH CUT TO:, for effect. You are generally going to want to leave out transition any time you find yourself rapidly cutting between scenes when adding them in will noticeably disrupt the flow of the sequence in question. This is particularly true for chase or montage scenes.

Chapter 2: Television Screenwriting Considerations

The format for television shows differs depending on how long they are supposed to run. Hour-long dramas are written up much like a movie screenplay, however, there are always breaks for act changes. Meanwhile, sitcoms and other, shorter, television shows are written a little differently which means their scripts have different formats to discern what they are supposed to be. The biggest difference between television and movie screenplays is that the level of standardization between genres, or even varying shows is far less well-defined. There are still going to have some hard and fast rules, however, which means the first thing you are going to want to do before you write a spec script is to read several scripts for the show you are going to be writing for so that you get a feel for what makes it unique.

Nevertheless, there are going to be some similarities in this field as well, and it is important that you understand what they are to ensure you get off on the right foot. One thing that is never going to change is the structure of the show in question. A 30-

minute television show is 22 minutes of content and 8 minutes of advertising (in general) and an hourlong show is typically 45 minutes of content and 15 minutes of commercials. The breaks need to be located in the right spots, which means the act breaks, with two or three additional breaks, depending on the network, for hourlong shows.

Drama

When it comes to writing drama, a good rule of thumb is to start every scene already in progress and make sure to move on to the next too early as opposed to too late. Additionally, you are going to want to be extremely selective when it comes to the scenes you do include, each one will need to either develop your characters or advance your plot, there is little room for anything else. The scenes that are going to end on commercial breaks should end on points of high dramatic tension, even if it is not integral to the plot as a whole. Above all you are going to want to keep your focus on showing, rather than telling.

Common types of dramas: There are several major types of dramas that tend to get produced, this is not to say that nothing else is ever going to get on the air, they are just the evergreen types of shows you can always expect to find somewhere on the dial. The first is the procedural, while this was once largely classified to police shows, there are now countless variations on the traditional solve a mystery in an hour formula, and you can find everything from medical to supernatural procedurals on television these days. The next type is the workplace drama, where there is equal focus on the jobs the characters do as well as on their personal lives.

After the success of Ga*me of Thrones*, the genre drama went from a small niche to big business. These types of shows typically blend fantasy or science fiction with more grounded characters and interpersonal stories. Finally, there are dramas found on premium cable channels, which can fall into any of the categories, but typically deal in much more extreme content matter and also don't need to worry about the traditional act breaks found in non-premium scripts.

Formatting: When it comes to formatting an hourlong script, if you don't have any sample material to look at, you can safely assume that it will be formatted in the same way a feature script would be, more or less, with the biggest difference being the act breaks. Don't forget, the average page of script is assumed to be about one minute, and the average script tends to come in at no more than 60 pages.

The first page, the cover page, that you provide should include the name of the show above the title of the episode above the writer's name. The next page will be the title name and it should include the same information as the cover page as well as your contact information printed below it.

The average episode is broken up into a teaser, which sets the stage for the episode and is what the viewer will see before the title sequence. The rest of the script will then be broken into four acts. Again, this is only an estimate as there are numerous shows that alter this format in one way or another, the best choice is always going to be tracking down a sample script from the show in question if you hope to be taken seriously.

Each act is going to be given a numerical designation and center at the top of the page that starts the act. Broadly speaking, both Act One and Act 1 are acceptable, just ensure that you are consistent throughout. Likewise, the end of each act should by bookended by End Act _. This should be two lines below the final line of text from the act, bolded and centered. FADE or CUT may be used to end a scene, but this is not required. A simple scene slug will do instead. Each new act should then start fresh at the top of a new page.

The average page breakdown per section works out as follows

Teaser: Between two and four pages

Act one: Between 14 and 15 pages

Act two: Between 14 and 15 pages

Act three: Between 14 and 15 pages

Act four: Between 14 and 15 pages

Tag: Between one and two pages

Total: Between 59 and 66 pages

Narrative structure: Broadly speaking, you are going to want to follow a standard three act structure for your script, the first act should set up the goal for the episode and the end of the first act will generally end with them failing to reach some sort of instant gratification. The second act will further complicate whatever it is that the main character is trying to do, while simultaneously raising the stakes. The end of this act will find the character at their lowest point for the entire episode.

Act three typically begins with something that renews the character's resolve and pushes them to get right to the point where they are going to attempt to overcome their obstacle. Finally, act four resolves everything, though the amount to which this is the case is going to be determined by whether or not the episodes are designed for standalone or serialized viewing.

As a general rule, you can expect the average modern series to include the main plot as well as two subplots that all take place at the same time. The main story is the A plot, the B plot is then the more involved of the two subplots while the C plot, also known as the runner, is typically limited to character building moments. These typically occur about three times throughout the episode. If your subplots are going to be referencing specific details from other plotlines of the television show in question, you will need to indicate where in the series continuity it takes place on the title page.

Sitcoms

The first thing you need to understand about writing situation comedies, is that you already need to be adept at telling jokes in order to succeed in the medium. Specifically, you need to concern yourself with timing as if a joke is executed poorly, especially on the page without a comedic actor to save it, it will fall flat every time.

Multicamera: When considering writing a sitcom script, the first thing you will need to consider is if the show you are considering writing a script for is filmed in the multicamera or single camera mindset. In general, you can expect a multicamera shows to have two acts while single camera shows will more often have three.

The general format for a multicamera show is as follows:

FADE IN: this should always be written in capital letters and underlined.

SCENE the scene should be numbered, capitalized and underlined with two spaces above and below it.

Slug the slug should always be underlined .

(Character list) the character list should be written directly underneath the slug and is used to tell the reader which characters are going to be in the scene. It should be encapsulated inside a parenthesis.

DESCRIPTIONS AND ACTIONS both required actions and relevant descriptions are always capitalized, don't forget to keep these to only plot specific requirements.

CHARACTER INTROS this should always be written in capital letters and underlined.

CAMERA INSTRUCTIONS, SPECIAL EFFFECTS AND SOUND EFFECTS this should always be written in capital letters and underlined.

CHARACTER NAMES AND DIALOUGE these should always be written in capital letters and double spaced.

(PERSONAL DIRECTION) this will appear within lines of dialogue, in all capital letters and enclosed in a parenthesis.

The first page after the cover and title page of average sitcom script will start with the name of the show written in capital letters, exactly six lines down from the top of the page and surrounded by quotation marks. Six lines below this you will want to center ACT ONE followed by A on the next line, which indicates the scene, also centered. 8 lines underneath this you will then write FADE IN: so that it aligns with a 1.4-inch margin. This should be followed by the list of characters that is going to appear in the scene. Each page should be numbered and also include the letter corresponding to the scene in question.

The second scene, and each additional scene will then start on a new page. 21 lines down from the top of the page you will put the scene designation, centered. Six lines below that you will then write the slug. Each act will also begin on a new page. When you are writing dialogue, you are going to want to make it double spaced to ensure it is easy to read. When you write stage direction, ensure you do so in all capital letters in order to more easily distinguish them from the dialogue. Each page should contain plenty of white space to ensure actors have space to write their own notes. In general, the following page breakdown should apply.

Teaser: Between one and two pages

Act one: Between 13 and 20 pages, depending on if the story has two or three acts

Act two: Between 13 and 20 pages, depending on if the story has two or three acts

Act three: Between 0 and 13 pages, depending on if the story has two or three acts

Tag: Between one and three pages

Total: Between 40 and 48 pages

Single camera: Single camera shows are typically going to be formatted more like dramas, though again, specific shows may vary. Even if they have commercial breaks, they may not have a traditional three act structure, especially if the entire season is serialized. When writing dialogue, as well as stage direction, you are going to want to make sure that both are single-spaced. Additionally, each character should have their name written in all capital letters the first time they are introduced onscreen. These scripts are typically the tightest of the three, rarely coming in at more than 32 pages in length.

Additional Tips to Keep In Mind

When writing for a sitcom, above all else you need to nail the tone as well as the voice of each character on the show you are writing a script for. The people who will be reading spec scripts know their shows inside and out and they will respond better to those they can tell know it just as well.

Your spec script should be thought of as your portfolio, resume and calling card all in one. As such, you better make sure it is great if you ever hope to get your foot in the door. In addition to being a tight, well-written story, your script needs to be completely free of all errors, if grammar isn't your strong suit, get someone else to edit your script for you. A lack of concern over the little things won't reflect well overall and could easily be the deciding factor between you and another aspiring screenwriter.

In general, you are going to want to stay away from writing a pilot before you have even landed a job in the industry as pilots from unknowns are rarely picked up. With that being said, however, if you have a great idea for a show, write the pilot episode and then write two or three more. By this point your characters will be more well-established and you can show the reader what your average episode is going to be like. This is crucial as the early episodes of many shows are spent establishing character relationships and interactions, leaving less time for traditional activities and jokes and leading to scripts that seem limp.

    Avoid using parentheticals whenever possible. Only leave them in if they clearly enhance the dialogue in a specific way. One of the only acceptable times is when the parenthetical will explain body language that will indicate that the character is saying one thing while clearly meaning something else. Likewise, you are going to want to avoid unnecessary explanations, if you can't make the scene work without explaining it, you should cut it, period. Finally, avoid adding scenes just to fill space, if you can fill out a full-length script with useful content it's time to go back to the drawing board.

Chapter 3: How to Create Characters

When it comes to writing a compelling screenplay, the first thing you that is likely going to come to you is going to be the basic outline of the plot. In order to ensure that this basic idea matures organically into a fully fleshed-out screenplay, the first thing you are going to want to do is more fully consider the characters that are going to be going with you on the adventure you are creating. You will find that getting to know your characters more intimately will make the process of actually connecting the dots on the story much more manageable.

You are not just going to want to only focus on creating a protagonist, you are going to want to consider who are going to be the main characters of your story, both protagonists and antagonists, and write character biographies as well. In fact, this is encouraged, especially if you are writing a feature length screenplay. You want a solid backstory and a solid foundation for writing your character into your story. This is a great way to create a very strong character that will draw the audience's attention until the very end.

Always remember the Theory of Illumination. This theory states that every character reflects on your main character. Their relationships, and their development, eventually lead them to your main character. While giving every character a fully-developed backstory on screen is not recommended, knowing the details of a character's life will make them easier to write for in addition to making them seem more well-rounded as a whole.

This means that you aren't going to want to flesh out all of your character bios in a single evening, you need to spend some time to really think each of your characters through. Take a few days where you spend a few hours to think about your characters, this time should be spent without distractions. No phones, no TV, no music, just you and your thoughts, because you want your character to be authentic, not a copy of a distraction that sticks in your mind. You want a truly original person, not a second-rate copy of someone else's character.

Then, you just start writing. Write anything that you feel is relevant to your character's development. Just let your character grow, and pretty much create themselves, with only the manipulation of the outline you have decided on. This is called free association. Free associating is where you let the words take you wherever, and you merely go along for the ride. This allows you to ensure that your character is not too stiff. You want your character to be real, not forced.

This is not say that everything you write during this period is going to be usable, and indeed much of it may be garbage. However, if you can successfully manage to channel your character for this process you never know what useful information you may end up discovering.

You want to follow every major aspect of your character, true, but you cannot neglect the small things that add up to make your character truly who they are. Remember, people are not made up of only the defining moments in their lives, they are also made up of all of the little, seemingly insignificant moments inbetween. You could possibly do a portion where you outline what their day looks like from the time they wake up, to the time they go to sleep. This will help you better establish the type of person your character will be as well.

If you find an area in your character's life, and you are not sure exactly which way to proceed, let the cards fall where they may. If you are still unsure, do a little research, and go from there. You want to know everything about your character, but you can also be surprised where the words take you. Remember, if you don't like what you come up with you can always scrap it later. When writing your script you should only be focused on creating the best story possible, not with how long the process takes you.

Write! Do not worry about if other people will love it, because if you do not, then no one will. You have to first and foremost be able to stand behind your screenplay one hundred percent. Otherwise, it will not be taken seriously. As the quality of your overall screenplay is going to be dependent on the strength of your characters, it equally stands to reason that you need to love them first, before you worry about anything else.

It is important to create dynamic characters and to keep yourself in line with how you want your screenplay to go. The character has to fall in line with what you want to achieve, and yet they also have to bring a certain element to the table as well. They have to create a little bit of chaos, while also maintaining the peace so to speak.

Imagine you are walking a tightrope. You have to have precision balance. That is what making a character is like. You have to have some flaws as no one wants to root for a character that is perfect. However, too many flaws will make your character seem like a mess, and unless your character is actually a mess, you want them to be relatable. So, you have to walk that tightrope between peace and chaos. This is harder than most people think. As it becomes too easy to make a character extremely flawed, or completely perfect. It becomes too easy to fall to one side or the other, and you have to stay in the middle. It is okay to teeter a few times, but you have to pull your balance back up and continue on.

If you are not able to do so, you will find that the whole story veers out of control, and that can make your screenplay less than desirable. This is what you want to avoid for a plethora of reasons, but the first being that you

Here are my top 5 tips for writing stronger characters into your screenplay:

Make your character likable early on: You have to make your character someone that the audience wants to spend at least ninety minutes with. This means you have to make them likable from the get-go. Even if you think the character is interesting, if they are not very positive, or they are annoying, the audience will lose interest before you get to the good parts of the character.

You want the audience to be able to identify with the character because that is what draws their interest in. The main character should be written as the protagonist, this way the main person is not a self-serving, negative drawback to the screenplay, unless the entire purpose of the screenplay is to chronicle their downfall or their redemption. In general, however, people want to see the negative characters portrayed as the antagonist. This way there is some balance between good and bad though, typically, good will win out in the end.

Your character does not have to be perfect, they just have to have some redeeming qualities. These qualities will help your character reach out to the audience in a way that keeps them interested. You can do this by making the dialogue witty and conversational. You can make them do a kind act in the beginning, such as saving a cat from a tree. In fact, there is an entire screenwriting book, entitled *Save the Cat* for just that reason. Regardless of the setup you choose, you just have to make sure that you set the tone for a likable character early on in the story. This is important, because if you do not, you may find that you lose your audience's interest before even grabbing a hold of it properly.

If you have a character that maybe does not have the best qualities, then it is important to include other, worse, characters to make him seem better in comparison. For example, if you have a character that may be in prison, you want to make him better than the other prisoners. Your character does not have to be a saint, just better than the others, and more relatable than a villain. They have to have a sense of purpose about them, to attract the audience to the plot line, and help them retain their interest until the very end. A complex character cannot get lost in his flaws.

Build realistic & detailed characters: While the character is who your person is, characterization is what they are. One is the true deep soul of the character, the other is the shallower, facade that they present to the rest of the world. For example, you could have a lonely woman who just wants someone to love as a character, but her characterization could be a CEO of a company who acts like she does not need anything from anyone. This is characterization. Sometimes the two are similar, and sometimes they are polar opposites. Like a hard, edgy teen is truly a softy on the inside. These contrasts, when revealed, make for a more detailed, believable characters, and a better storyline. People love to be surprised and love finding out more about the characters in a story. So, you have to make sure that you detail their characterization precisely. You want to make sure that you put some emphasis on who they are, but also what they are as well – the inside and the outside.

Writing strong characterization is important on so many levels. First off, a realistically depicted character will add a lot of realism to your piece. I cannot count how many times I've seen the same generic antagonist in a film that had zero original characterization, which ultimately completely diminished their importance in the film. But even outside of just adding realism to the characters, it can also help you as a writer to tell your story more intuitively and dramatically.

Just like you want to write a character biography, you also want to create characterization sheets. These help you discern what your character will be like throughout most of the screenplay. You can do this quickly, through another round of free association. Give your character choices, as if they were living, breathing, individuals. It is important for you to be free flowing with your characters so that they feel authentic and realistic. If you try to force your character to completely match someone who inspires you, the character will feel forced. Let the character speak to you. Which, coincidentally, brings us directly up to the next tip.

Let your character make the decisions for you: **Many** writers feel that their screenplay has to be completely mapped out before they even begin writing, and while it is important for you to make sure that you have the structure outlined, it is equally important to let your characters breathe, otherwise the setting will feel fake and forced, which is the opposite of what you want.

Rather than forcing your character into a box that you have neatly outlined before you have even touched the first sentence, you should let your character make their own decisions. This may sound silly because you are the writer, but the truth is, once you have spent enough time with your characters this will seem much more reasonable. Once you have spent enough time chronicling their likes and dislikes, you will find that you will be able to easily picture what they would do when confronted with a specific decision. You want them to come alive and come off the page, which means you have to let the characters take control sometimes. This allows the scene to feel more realistic, and give it more depth.

While your character may be an extension of yourself, they are also a separate entity from you as well and should be treated as such. With that being said, however, if you give a character a trait that you share with them, then it becomes much easier to anticipate how they would act in a given situation as you can use your own experiences as a point of reference.

If you have already created a character biography and a characterization sheet, then this should be an easy thing to do. You should know your character inside out, and as your character grows, how they will make their way through the story should become clear. So, while you might have thought the character could go one way, you may be surprised when you get to that point, and find that another solution suddenly makes more sense.

Likewise, you are going to want your characters to grow organically which means letting them change as the story dictates, as opposed to forcing them to remain in a predetermined box. Not only will this do a disservice to the character overall, it is unsatisfying for an audience to leave a character exactly where they started, either mentally, emotionally or physically, unless that fact is central to the overall plot. You want them to be like real people, because they will be portrayed by real people, and your target audience will be real people, so you have to make sure that your character has depth.

Approach the early drafts with an open mind, and that will help you build an organic, relatable character. Even if it means you have to change a lot because one choice changes everything.

You will find that the more you let your character choose, the more realistic the story will feel, and the more interest the story will garner. This is what you are looking for because you want the character to draw the audience in. It is important that you write some serious choices in as well, as a screenplay without real consequences is likely lacking in dramatic tension as well.

Give your character compelling dialogue: Dialogue was touched on earlier, but it is important enough to warrant further consideration. All of your characters need to have a strong dialogue. This will establish who they are within their first few lines. Even if they do not have a lot of lines, the ones that they have should be solid, and discerning.

So much can be conveyed by the simple use of dialogue. Accent can determine where the character is from. Their sentence structure can determine how educated they are. The tone of voice can determine if they are introverted or extroverted. All of this and more can be shown just by how the character's lines are written.

Something as simple as a scene where a character is running errands, and talking to the people they meet can tell a lot about the character. This may seem odd, but it is true because they are showing a piece of themselves in their everyday life.

Even though the narrative films are fiction, people want them to seem as realistic as they possibly can. This is because people like what they can relate to. They want to be able to feel a connection to a character, even if it is an animated character. Dialogue is a great way to do that.

Compelling dialogue is not always a lot of dialogue. You could have a character that speaks very little, and yet they could be a very dynamic character. How you set up their dialogue really sets the tone for how they are portrayed. You have to make sure that no matter how many lines of dialogue a character has, they are set up to portray a depth to that character.

Something that you want to stay away from is one-dimensional dialogue. This is where all of your characters speak the same. Even if they are all from the same area and same family, every person speaks differently. While similar characters may have similar dialogue, they should also have their own unique characteristics in their dialogue. This will help you discern the different people when the storyline starts speeding up. If you have all the same dialogue, the characters will blend into one another.

#5 – Think like an actor and give your character a point of view

One of the most important things to think about is the character's point of view. As the writer, you see everything, but the main character does not. You have to make sure that you are writing with the character's point of view to ensure that confusion does not set in by the character knowing something that would be impossible for them to know. This clutters things up and makes it hard to keep the scenes straight.

If you are laughing at this tip, you need it the most. You cannot just slap a character down all willy-nilly, you have to put some thought into it. You want a character that will be easy to figure out so that the actor can do the character the justice they deserve.

The most important reason to write a strong point of view is that it gives a line for the story to follow. The audience needs to understand where the character stands, and if the character does not have a solid point of view, then this gets harder to do, and it gets frustrating for the audience, the actors, and everyone involved in the creation of the work you have worked so hard on.

Have you ever seen *Forrest Gump?* In the movie, the main character, Forrest Gump, has a very strong point of view. In fact, the entire movie is told from his point of view. You can see where he stands on life, love, and running. This is what you are looking for in a character, even if it is not written in first person point of view.

There are so many screenplays that lack this concept. These are the ones that often get tossed out because no one wants to be confused for ninety minutes. They want to be able to easily follow the character.

Some scenes are drawn out longer than necessary because the character does not have a strong point of view, which causes the scenes to run around in circles. This makes it harder to follow, and more confusing for the audiences that you may have.

A test to see if you are heading in the right direction is to see if you could cut the scene down to no more than two pages. While some scenes need a lot of dialogue, there are still ways to cut it down to make those two pages, and if you cannot do that, then perhaps you have to reevaluate the scene and the character's strength in their point of view. It is best to do this in the editing stages to see what needs to be changed.

What else can we do?

There is no set formula for how to write a character, but if you follow these tips, you will be off to a good start. It is important that you find what works for you because you have to have a solid character for your storyline to move forward.

In fact, all of your characters need to be strong, so that they move the story along smoothly. A bad character is like a speed bump. It interrupts a steady pace and can be frustrating if there is a lot of them.

There are other tips that you can find from other writers as well. Spend some time with your local writer's guild, or go to the library. This will help you immensely to find yourself and find the character you are looking to create. You have to have a solid grasp on your character, for them to flourish.

Go out in the world, and people watch. You can get some ideas for character traits you would like to have in a character. Walmart, the mall, the park. These are all great places to find interesting characters.

Chapter 4: Creating a Rough Draft

Most contracts that you enter into will give you three months maximum from the pitch to come up with a rough draft. Three months may seem like a good amount of time, but it is actually not a lot of time. You have to work swiftly, and efficiently to get your rough draft out in time. Otherwise, you may lose your shot.

Something that helps is to remember that screenplays are time-related. While a novel can be as long or as short as you would like, most feature films run between ninety minutes and two hours. This makes it harder, and easier at the same time. It gives you an idea of how many pages to write but also makes it that much more restrictive to write with a deadline, and a page limit as well. You want to make sure that you streamline the process, to make things go a lot easier.

Getting a good workflow will give you a good storyline. You do not want to seem like you rushed the development. Here are some ideas for a good workflow.

Develop the story idea:

Before you can come up with a story, you must first start with an idea. You cannot just slap words on a page and call it a screenplay. Go somewhere that inspires you, and get an idea for the story from start to finish.

Create the pitch:

Then you have to create the pitch that will give you an idea of how the story will flow. Start with the five finger pitch. This is where you list some major events on one hand. These events once explained should flow nicely. If they do not go do some more thinking. If they do, then you can move on to the two-handed pitch which is just more events that flow smoothly. Once this is complete, you have a solid foundation for your storyline.

Give it structure:

This is like adding the walls to a house. You have to add more turning points, and supporting events. You want to be able to hold the story up, and by giving it structure, then you can have a full blown story coming your way soon.

The importance of structure is that it keeps the entire story from just falling apart at the seams. If you do not have a strong structure of your house, it will fall down. Same with a story.

Build a full story:

Also known as a synopsis, this is where you get all of the major events mapped out. Basically, the synopsis is a one page summary of the entire story. It is the story without all of the minor details and dialogue. Once this is done, you can move onto the next step, which brings you closer to actually writing the rough draft.

Create a beat sheet:

This is a basic outline that will help you keep track of where the story is at, and where it will go next. The outline does not need to be really detailed, it is just a little bullet point list that you can check off as you pass each point in your writing once you finally get to writing your script.

The importance of a beat sheet is to ensure that you are keeping up with the storyline, and moving at the proper pace. Otherwise, you will find that you are stuck, and being stuck can cost you precious time.

Write the script (finally):

Woohoo! It is finally time to get to script writing. You have to make sure that your outline is complete first, and then you can get down to business. There are a lot of software out there that will help you, as they already have the formatting ready for you. Some also have tips and tricks for writing a good script as well. If you are not sure of your abilities, there are software out there that will proofread your script as well for you, though they are a little more costly.

As you are writing, you may find that you need to tweak what you had previously written. Do not go deleting anything yet, instead, create a list of things that need to be fixed, and when you go to edit your rough draft afterward, then you can create an edited rough draft later on. This way you can keep things on track, and get your first rough draft punched out.

Do not delete your original rough draft. It should be kept as your first draft in case you need to go back and reference changes. Once you have edited all of the additional things into your script, you can celebrate.

NEXT STEPS:

The next step is to get your rough draft to the company you have a contract with. They will look it over, and tell you if they like it, and what they feel needs work. Then you can get to editing.

Chapter 5: Editing a Screenplay

Have you ever wondered why a character is rarely seen eating, drinking water, or going to the bathroom unless it has significance to the storyline? The reason these things are rarely portrayed is that this would be too much information, and would drag the story on too long.

In any storytelling form, you have to edit the life of a character in some way. This will keep the storyline moving, and keep it from getting tedious. Bathroom breaks, minor incidences, and repetitive action are generally not important in a storyline, so if you have too much of these, they should be edited out.

Before a screenplay is produced, there are many ways a writer can edit their screenplays. Whether it be through editing and rearranging scenes, juxtaposition, and cutting the fat. All of these are resources that will help the editing process move forward.

Juxtaposition is important to use in any form of art, and screenwriting does not escape its grasp. Just by changing the juxtaposition of scenes, you can give the story an entirely different feel.

This can be used in one scene or two scenes, or depending on how many you need to use it on to help get the point across.

Crosscut and parallel action are two points of juxtaposition that are most commonly used in writing, and they are found to be very effective in creating different tones for different scenes, which is what writers want to achieve.

For instance, a very fun moment cut directly into a boring moment can accentuate that boredom through contrast.

Juxtaposition is a word that is not overlooked in any editing class. It is useful in so many areas, from writing to cinematography, and stage preparation. Prop work as well. The contrast it creates can be useful in setting a tone and creating a mood. This makes it less necessary for words to set the tone, which will leave you more words for important things.

Sometimes, you get so attached to your story that you do not want to cut anything, but the unnecessary parts are important to cut because they just slow the production down. It is important to cut them before they get to production if possible because you do not want to waste more time than you absolutely have to.

Some directors are more spontaneous though. They want you to leave it all in, and they will see how it works as it is being filmed. However, if you cannot get a scene to work when you are writing it, it is still best to leave it out.

However, if you are lower budget, you should make all of the necessary cuts before production, because any delays can cost a lot of money. If you do not have that much money, to begin with, then you will have a hard time recovering.

Removing weaker scenes do not just help production, they help the budget as well. Every page of the script costs money, and if you cut the weaker scenes that wouldn't make the cut anyway, then you save the money it would take to produce them.

Cutting scenes post-production also causes a lot of problems with continuity in a piece as well, because there is not enough time to smooth out the edges.

The continuity of a film is really important. Without that continuity, it will feel like someone gave a twelve-year-old a camera and told them to make a movie.

It is important to take the lighting into consideration as well. Consider how the light will affect the mood. So when editing, you have to pay close attention to the lighting to make sure it stays consistent. Fix it if you need to because the wrong lighting could set the wrong mood, which would shut your whole production down. If you do not want that you will make sure to specify the time of day in every scene.

Not only does the light change, but your character may also change as well. If a lot of time progresses, your character cannot stay the same the entire time. You have to make sure that you have made note of the changes as the film progresses.

The visuals are usually clear-cut, but if scenes need to be cut in post-production, that can disrupt the visuals. If several scenes need cut, then you may find that certain scenes need to be reshot to fix the visuals. This is another reason to focus on editing closely.

When editing, it is important to keep in mind the order of the scenes to ensure that the continuity is there. If something needs to be switched around, make sure to adjust it accordingly, so that the visuals are smooth, and there are no visual speed bumps when you hit production. Because it becomes a lot harder to fix on the spot then, and you want a smooth transition to have a successful film. Visuals are very important, and it is important to remember that.

Another part of editing is to make sure that you note the transitions. Every film has to have transitions between scenes so that they flow smoothly. Otherwise, you would have to add a whole lot more information. These transitions are a lot easier to add in the editing process than the post-production days. So make sure to make a note of the transitions before it becomes harder to add them.

Another reason to make sure everything is solid in editing is that there can be unwanted interpretations if you have to cut scenes in post-production. Doing so between similar scenes can create confusion, and doing so between contrasting scenes can be jarring and dramatic. This can be used to say something if it is intentional. However, if it is not intentional, you risk saying something to the audience that you never meant to say, which can leave them confused.

Also, directors do not like to be told how to do their job, so avoid technical directions in your script. Instead be subtle in telling the director where the camera should be pointed. Instead of saying "Point camera to the west." You could say "The main character looked off into a beautiful sunset, contemplating the meaning of life. Since the sun sets in the west, the camera will point west.

Editing can save you from a lot of issues later on in life and ensures smoother transitions as you head into production. It is important to make sure you edit out all of the kinks to save money when it comes time to shoot the film. Now if only taxes could be edited out of our lives.

Chapter 6: Tips for Success

While there are a wide variety of reasons that you might want to be a screenwriter, if you are hoping to do so in order to adopt a shorter, less stressful, work week you may be extremely disappointed. In fact, successful screenwriters are often extremely disciplined, dedicated individuals who have trained themselves to create something from nothing, day end and day out in order to ensure they always have something productive in the pipeline. While what works out to be an effective process for each writer is going to differ, sometimes dramatically, the most successful all typically have a number of habits in common that make the task before them more manageable. These are outlined here, in hopes that at least a few of them will inspire you to write more successfully in the future.

They have a reason to write: The best screenplays, especially those written by first time screenwriters are written with a specific purpose in mind, by writers with a driving desire to tell a specific story. This doesn't mean that your motivations for telling your story need to be pure as the driven snow, after all, entertaining others is as good of reason as any. The important thing is that you have a reason that is strong enough to drive you to continue trying to tell your story no matter how hard the going is going to get, and it is likely to be quite difficult from time to time.

Regardless of the motives that you have for writing, you need to be passionate about it if you ever hope to find true success. Don't feel ashamed if part of the reason that you want to write a successful screenplay has something to do with egotism, remember, the goal isn't to make yourself want to write a screenplay that will change the world, it is to find what drives you to write, and in this case egotism is as useful of a reason as any. Everyone wants recognition to some degree, and if you want to write for revenge, glory, fame, money, power, or simply to prove that you can, then you can harness that energy and use to make you a better writer, ensuring you actually see the screenplay through in the process.

They demand the best from themselves: When you first start writing your screenplay, it is perfectly acceptable to leave in placeholder scenes and text, from time to time, just to ensure you make it through to the end in one piece. With that being said, it is important to keep in mind that the spec script your produce is going to be the one, and often only, thing that people in the industry look at when they decide if they are going to give you your big break which means that settling for anything less that absolute perfection is akin to throwing away all the time that you ultimately spend on your screenplay.

As such, it is important to never settle with your first draft, your second or even your fourth. You are going to want to go through the entire thing with a fine-tooth comb until the story is as tight and compelling as possible. While this is only going to ever take you so far, it will at least ensure that the screenplay that you send in is the most accurate indication of what you are capable of as possible.

At the same time, you are going to want to make a conscious effort to stop making changes at the point where the work, as presented, speaks for itself as you can always find something to tweak or change. Eventually you are going to need to have the confidence in yourself to put the work out there and, hopefully, start receiving feedback on it. If you don't practice restraint, your screenplay will likely end up feeling overwrought, as you will have overthought whatever spark was there to begin with into oblivion.

They write what they like, and what they know: While anyone can have an idea for any type of story, and that story might be unique, or relatable, enough to resonate with the world at large, you will typically find that it is much easier to write about things that you have first-hand knowledge about and also much easier to keep at it if you like whatever it is that you are writing. Again, it is perfectly acceptable to get into the screenwriting business for its potential for lucrative gains, this in no way means that you can't enjoy the process along the way. What's more, if you find the story in your screenplay exciting, the odds are high that those around you are going to feel the same way.

Likewise, when it comes to writing what you know, this doesn't mean writing a movie about being an accountant for an accounting firm, unless you have an idea that will make the process seem roughly 2,000 percent more exciting than the topic naturally seems to the average person. Rather, adding in touches from your every day life can make certain characters more believable, or giving one of your hobbies to a character can make them seem more three-dimensional. What's more, you never know when something from, even a seemingly boring job, can provide you with the one realistic, but unexpected, fact that you need to tie the whole plot together.

They set goals: If you have never before found yourself sitting in front of a blank screen, with all the freedom in the world in front of you, only to find yourself looking for any excuse to be anywhere else, then the idea of setting writing goals to ensure you actually finish your screenplay may seem unnecessary. The first time you make the decision to bolt rather than face down your writer's block, however, you will realize just how vital setting goals can be. Likewise, if you have never written anything substantial before, then you may find yourself doing all the research you need to complete your screenplay, only to find that you never actually get any closer to generating a truly finished product.

As such, you should start by setting goals for your pre-writing process, including generating characters, a basic plot synopsis, world building elements etc. You should give yourself plenty of time for the more free-form nature of this part of the process, though you should have a firm deadline when you want to begin the actual writing to ensure that fleshing out your characters doesn't end up taking years to finish.

When it comes to writing the first draft, you are going to want to make a concentrated effort to write for at least an hour a day, at least five days a week, and also spend some time on the sixth day coming up with a general idea of where the end of the next week should find you. Writing every day will help to ensure that you don't lose the flow of the story as it can be hard to recapture lost momentum once it has slipped away. While writing for a set period of time is fine, you will find that you will be more productive still if you task yourself with writing a set number of pages each day. This will ensure that you maintain your productivity, rather than just waiting out the clock on days where inspiration takes longer to strike. In addition to page goals, you are going to want to have a general idea of where you want to the story to go next, so you can steer things in that direction.

When it comes to editing, you are going to want to set hourly goals, as it is difficult to say just how much work you will get done per session as it is going to vary so dramatically. When it comes to setting an overall timeline for completion, you are going to want to give yourself enough time to ensure you don't rush, but not so much that you don't feel obligated to make daily progress. When setting these goals, it is important to keep in mind that they are not taking place in a vacuum. Writing for three or four hours every day is an admirable goal, and likely one that is completely unrealistic if you already have a fulltime job. It is important to set goals that are achievable as failing to do so can harm your morale and making finishing your screenplay harder than it already is.

Finally, the overall length of your timeline isn't important, as there is no standard amount of time it should take to create a quality screenplay. The most important thing overall, is that setting a schedule will help you to make finishing your screenplay a priority which means you are going to be far more likely to finish it than you otherwise would. Remember, your screenplay could be your shot at the bigtime, but the only way you will ever know for sure is if you actually finish it.

Conclusion

Hopefully, you learned a lot about writing a screenplay from this book. It was filled with plenty of tips on how to proceed. This is important because you cannot just jump in.

Now, you can go out, and start working on your screenplay. This book can be your guide if you whenever get stuck.

Thank you and good luck!

Made in the USA
Las Vegas, NV
08 October 2023